THE LAST SKIN

THE LAST SKIN

Barbara Ras

PENGUIN POETS

PENGUIN BOOKS

Published by the Penguin Group

Penguin Group (USA) Inc., 375 Hudson Street, New York, New York 10014, U.S.A.

Penguin Group (Canada), 90 Eglinton Avenue East, Suite 700, Toronto, Ontario, Canada M4P 2Y3

(a division of Pearson Penguin Canada Inc.)

Penguin Books Ltd, 80 Strand, London WC2R ORL, England

Penguin Ireland, 25 St Stephen's Green, Dublin 2, Ireland (a division of Penguin Books Ltd)

Penguin Group (Australia), 250 Camberwell Road, Camberwell, Victoria 3124, Australia

(a division of Pearson Australia Group Pty Ltd)

Penguin Books India Pvt Ltd, 11 Community Centre, Panchsheel Park, New Delhi - 110 017, India

Penguin Group (NZ), 67 Apollo Drive, Rosedale, North Shore 0632, New Zealand

(a division of Pearson New Zealand Ltd)

Penguin Books (South Africa) (Pty) Ltd, 24 Sturdee Avenue, Rosebank, Johannesburg 2196, South Africa

Penguin Books Ltd, Registered Offices:
80 Strand, London WC2R 0RL, England

First published in Penguin Books 2010

10   9   8   7   6   5   4   3   2   1

LIBRARY OF CONGRESS CATALOGING IN PUBLICATION DATA
Ras, Barbara.
The last skin / Barbara Ras.
p.   cm.—(Penguin poets)
ISBN 978-0-14-311697-4
I. Title.
PS3568.A637L37 2010
811'.54—dc22 2009053320

Printed in the United States of America
Set in Dante
Designed by Ginger Legato

For my mother, Helen E. Ras
December 24, 1914, to September 21, 2002
In memoriam

ACKNOWLEDGMENTS

Many thanks to the editors of the following magazines and publications, where the following poems first appeared, some in different versions and occasionally with other titles:

Callaloo, "Dear C"
Cincinnati Review, "An Oxcart and the Aroma of Hazelnuts" and "Blue Door"
Green Mountains Review, "Other Than Fullness"
In the Red/In the Black: Poems of Profit and Loss, ed. Philip Miller and Gloria
    Vando, "The Water, the Sand, the Embers"
Massachusetts Review, "Palm Reading"
The New Yorker, "Washing the Elephant"
Northwest Review, "Floating Islands"
Orion, "It Came Down Ice Last Night" and "A Book Said Dream and I Do"
Smartish Pace, "Manager of the Empty Hotel," "Town of Orphaned Teeth,"
    and "Windows on the Lake"
TriQuarterly, "Nothing Was Ever Better Than Before," "Impossible Dance,"
    and "Pigeons, A Love Poem"

Deep gratitude to the Artist Foundation of San Antonio, whose generous grant helped during the writing of this book.

Enduring thanks to: Alfred Rucker, Anna Zoë Rucker, Ellen Doré Watson, Emily Wheeler, Nan Cuba, Wendy Barker, Jenny Browne, Marianne Boruch, Jan Jarboe Russell, Andrew Porter, Jerry Winakur, Lee Robinson, Naomi Shihab Nye, Gerald Stern, Rebecca Solnit, George Nitchie, Michael Fischer, and Abe Louise Young.

Additional appreciation to Marian Haddad, Ignacio Magaloni, Assef Al-Jundi, Karen Kelley, Roberto Bonazzi, and Jim LaVilla-Havelin, for help along the path.

Special thanks to Betsy Rogers for a quiet haven in which to write.

With great admiration, huge thanks to Ellen Phelan for facilitating the use of her work *Applause* for the cover art.

To Paul Slovak and the rest of the team at Penguin, thank you for your invaluable support, terrific help with this book, and for your commitment to poetry.

CONTENTS

PART I

PART II: LAKE TITICACA

PART III

THE LAST SKIN

PART I

A BOOK SAID DREAM AND I DO

There were feathers and the light that passed through feathers.

There were birds that made the feathers and the sun that made the light.

The feathers of the birds made the air soft, softer

than the quiet in a cocoon waiting for wings,

stiller than the stare of a hooded falcon.

But no falcons in this green made by the passage of parents.

No, not parents, parrots flying through slow sleep

casting green rays to light the long dream.

If skin, dew would have drenched it, but dust

hung in space like the stoppage of

time itself, which, after dancing with parrots,

had said, Thank you. I'll rest now.

It's not too late to say the parrot light was thick

enough to part with a hand, and the feathers softening

the path, fallen after so much touching of cheeks,

were red, hibiscus red split by veins of flight

now at the end of flying.

Despite the halt of time, the feathers trusted red

and believed indolence would fill the long dream,

until the book shut and time began again to hurt.

THE WATER, THE SAND, THE EMBERS

Frailty everywhere, in the loops
of blood traveling 12,000 miles of veins a day,
and in the fluttering of prayer flags hung out
on a cold day that promised sun, but delivered
snow, all its flaky symmetry lost on impact.
Trembling in the cities, wavering between masks
and crutches, between Rabelais and Robespierre.
Harshness of light, bend of dark, the boots
of justice, trembling. Should I speak of bones
in a plot of purchased dirt, buried in dark
mahogany, itself in danger?
No matter what, at the wake
they'll say, "She looks good, doesn't she,"
death and disguise at a standoff so tense,
petals tremble.
And you, the last time you trembled—
was it like bird, beast, or fish? Or like
trees, the most agile of tremblers?
The water, the sand, the embers tremble.
When the sun angles at the right slant,
it finds us in our little cave, a few friends,
a late huddle, failure dancing around
our fragile fire, the fire we feed
with our nail bitings, our paper money,
our guilt, our worthless guilt, breath and more
breath, while beside ourselves, our shadows flicker,
in despair, in laughter, the same trembling.

DARK THIRTY

All year, death, after death, after death.
Then today look how majestically clouds float in the sky,
God putting on a show of tenderness, nothing like thoughts
that rise and drift in my mind, like flakes shaken
in a snow globe, and my brain laboring in its own night,
never feeling the punky starlight of dark thirty, the time
a friend said for us to meet and had to explain it was half an hour
after the first dark, when daylilies fold up and headlights
lead the way home, but maybe too early
to find the moon turning half its body away,
holding it hidden like the black side of a mirror, unseen
until it breaks, unexpectedly, the way grief
breaks over you when you've already given all you've got
and hands you tools you don't know how to use.

The blush of dark thirty turned bleak
when I heard about the O—
O dark thirty, military time for 12:30 a.m.,
hour of the deepest dark, when, if I'm awake,
as I often am, a storm of thoughts battle one another, now settling
unsettlingly on the ways we make war and flaunt it.
Take the Civil War double cannon on the lawn
of a city hall in the deep south, twinned so that two cannonballs
chained together kill two at a time, often decapitating.
And why did a small town, population 932, in rural New Hampshire,
import a ballistic missile to crown its village green?

Brecht's line floats up: "Pity the nation that needs heroes,"
but what to do with the guy pontificating on the Middle East,
telling me with the gravest authority—
that of stupidity—the reason for the strife there:
"Hatred is in the rocks."

NOW ALL THE FEARS

Not just falling down the stairs, but the stairs
    crumbling under your feet.
Not just the crack in the glass, but windows
    in shards under your feet.
Not just thieves at the door, but the door gone,
    a severed hand under your feet.
Not just bombs on the roof, but white phosphorus,
    so when you walk, burnt skin hisses under your feet.

Not just how long the food will last, but hunger
    as pointed as a weapon, its boot on your neck.
Not just kneeling empty of prayers, but face down
    in the dirt with a boot on your neck.
Not just the taste of dirt, but dirt mixed with the taste of blood,
    your teeth broken by the weight of a boot on your neck.
Not just the loss of love, but the loss of everything
    but hatred, its boot to your neck.

Now all the fears have mustered and with them a lust
    for boots, and necks under your feet.

TRAIN

All day the train
chases time, all night
time's shadow.
The train dreams
of solitude, fine light,
sometimes the vagaries,
sometimes the flood.
The train takes us,
yakkers, fish pickers,
toilers of sand, the man
carrying a bucket of snails,
the broken woman in a fur coat,
wayward ones in search of a lift,
an alley, the needle. The train
takes dreadlocks,
deadbeats, and born-agains,
and the lost friend, learning
to disappear so quickly
we don't see him go.
The train dreams, and scenes
flash by as they do when a life
meets its death,
the train's death stopping
and starting, pages ripped,
and ripped, and ripped.
Now exiles, hunger hanging
from them like flags,
and the girl, always the girl,
her head against the cold
window, weeping.
Here is the jailer, his cuffs
on fire, shirt cuffs, pant cuffs,
four rings of fire like ID bracelets.
The train holds us, propelled

by the grinding need
of its loins grinding.
All day the train chases
understanding, all night
understanding's ghost.

VOICES FROM THE CORNERS OF THE SKY

Some of us are leaving now.
Some of us have done our time.

Some of us were taller candles and had more burning to do.
"Poof," you said, and it was true, "Poof."

Maybe we loved you, but not always.
Maybe you loved us and it will never be done.

We're finished now with lost keys, the dust
of teeth grindings milled mostly at night.

The shimmering is falling off your names and the names
of things, the pots, the colors, the books that fed us.

Whatever language we take with us—the murmur
of flowers fallen face down in the mud, the drink's ice

chinking to seal the sunset, the exhalations at the end
of circling a place to lie down a dog makes, lying down—

think of it as one day coming back to you
in the rain's slow trickle down panes of glass.

Now, please. Let us go
like a meadow of balloons let loose to the sky.

SITKA CEMETERY

Skunk cabbage made chambers of air
I wandered in and out of.

Old headstones leaned every which way, evading the past
or falling forward toward full repose.

There was lace-carved stone, and a headless cherub's dress
draped over chubby toddler legs.

A metallic whirligig on a grave spun, then stilled,
then spun some more, in cahoots with the wind's gambol.

A worker holding a wire brush pointed out a secret raven's nest
in a towering tree and begged us not to tell.

Someone touched a slug the size of a cigar.
Someone else said, "Words are blankets."

The shadows of eagles made imperfect crosses on the ground,
and I confess I've crossed myself enough to last a lifetime.

If I had had a pencil, I would have broken it
in two and left one half on the grave of a mother, the other,
on the grave of a child.

SEVEN

1.

Mushrooms drying over the kitchen sink
in my grandparents' apartment, and my four-year-old
incredulity that their two bodies ugly with age
dared to go into the forest and bend down to the lure
of food that was one reach from fatal, though even
the good ones made a stench that filled my small blonde head
with worms.

2.

Pain like dice, like key numbers
on bones that some arrogant god
disdained to follow assembling the skeleton.
How else explain the body's migrating aches,
its rattling storm windows—the old kind
with wood frames that attached to the house with eye hooks
that every fall my father and his father hauled up from the cellar,
wrestling the green-framed glass between them,
while my brother and I in the living room built simple cages
with Tinkertoys, not for a minute thinking kids
might have bedrooms big enough
for two to play in at once.

3.

Adolescence, enough all by itself, but add
love, the first kind that peels you all the way away,
so that being naked was like entering a new realm
with a name like Aquitaine, its boundaries shifting,
its borders contested. I can tell you worlds

about his eyes, their pale mineral light
like the bluest of bays shining through the thinnest ice,
but the only words of his I remember were
"please kiss it."

4.

In this year, 2008, the ratio of Hummers to hybrids is 20 to 1,
and that word "hummer," not just inept, preposterous,
suggesting as it does the hummingbird, mere grams
of life on a blur of wings, carrying aloft the swiftest heartbeat,
the sheerest bones. My dead mother
used the word "humdinger,"
but never praised me for fear it would go to my head,
so that even now compliments run off me like rain
ran off the garage roof into the family rain barrel.
And weirdly, during my interminable childhood,
I never saw a single person approach that corner of the yard,
where the lingering rain imperceptibly
returned to sky.

5.

Yes, no, maybe—the unending cha-cha-cha
of consciousness.

6.

Consciousness, and with it more than a hundred billion neurons,
"firing," as they say, as it's said cluster bombs do on contact,
but which in fact *drop today, kill tomorrow*, littering
civilian ground with devices that look like
lawn darts, green baseballs, orange-striped soda cans.
Efficient, a single cluster weapon carries *hundreds of submunitions,*
each carrying *flying shards of steel*, enough to cover
football fields or be dispersed over an even wider area
up to 100 acres. An untold number of brains could fit into
100 acres, and in combination they could fire a zillion neurons,
which even a fool knows triggers a lot of thinking,
but what good is it, side by side with murderous toys,
bomblets ready to detonate *at the slightest touch.*
Where farmers work, explosions greet them in the fields.
Where children play, explosions end their curiosity.
The munitions draw people to them *almost mystically.*
Perhaps it's the *streamers*
that say party in every language.

7.

It was on my seventh birthday that I realized
all the candles my mother stuck into the cake
had been burned before.

8.

The number 8 on its side makes the sign for infinity.
You didn't expect me to stop at 7, did you?

SAY SOMETHING

Nights fall. Days fall harder.

Gravity conspires with snakes,

bells stop, the hearts of birds

pull dangerously

against their wings,

clocks—

who knows about the clocks.

The priest says, Time now

for shrouds, time now for crying,

kneelers lowered thunking

on the bare floor.

That sound,

that unintentionally

wounding sound.

Time now, the teacher says,

to take the vain out of glory,

sweep the cape off the land,

beg the taker to take us

up, not under.

The politician speaks.

Time now, he says,

for the knowing laugh,

not your silly, silly crying.

What more could he say,

looking away

while all the nails

back out of all their wood?

I would dream

if my dream knives

were different

from the stained dull blades

in the kitchen drawer.

I would pray

if not for the acoustics.

If there is a story here,

it is told in helpless,

helpless hand gestures,

the narrator forlorn,

and though barrels

arrive on time,

they arrive broken,

and after wine,

darkness

keeps pouring out.

WHERE LAND ENDS

Only the dullest insomniacs ignore the moon's light,

the purported rabbits drawn on its pocked face.

Focus, please, on the alabaster streaming through near space,

carrying waves, but not the smell of the rock.

Imagine that round confection above us guiding the tides.

And me? Haven't I spent a lifetime searching for the edge

between the landing and the sea, the edge that ends,

like vanity, at a new place depending on the day?

Atoms to oranges, breath to bubbles, circles to circles to

circles, the round and round of not sleeping stalks

the full dark dread of succumbing to dreams,

while I am tossed over and over by the ocean that holds me ransom.

NO MATTER WHAT

Waking from grief's labor,
its hell-bent maniacal
pursuit of bones,
begging for bones, some crux,
some crutch, some last lumber
or straw, I know the dark rack
of mourning will not rest
until I take them one by one, bone by bone,
which I will not do, all night I refuse,
not the marrow, no matter what
is begged of me, I will not
suck it out.

NOTHING WAS EVER BETTER THAN BEFORE

Nothing was ever better than before—then,
when music of Chopin, music of Mahler, and
Bartók, whose notes wanted to make even the bears
dance happily, despite their chains, their burnt paws.

Today the news, opening old sores, like chewing
pinecones—that most hand grenade of fruits—
so that when we taste, we taste bitter,
forgetting the flavor of truth, and when we speak,
our speech crawls on all fours.

No music in dreams. No moon, either.
But running, fleeing in ever slower motion
in the dark from people with knives who chase in ever faster
motion, their hunger whetted by the smell of knives,
the edges of blades as merciless as insects.

Memory asks me, *How did you get such answers*
from the places you went to ask?
In the same way, I say, a pianist played
pieces for one hand after the other was lost in the war,
yet he went on wrenching beauty from the iron of severance.

Nothing was ever better than before, walking
under tall, blameless trees, breathing their calm
and watching leaves drift like the last of anguish,
while we, grandly infatuated, lounged on a blanket to feed
ourselves with figs, foreign cheese, and Côtes du Rhône.

That too was a dream, that too was
before death crept close enough to lick my shoes,
before nature turned vengeful, before skulls
in orderly rows
filled a field from this edge of the photo

to the horizon, gleaming white
bone against black dirt,
all the eyes gone to a place where nothing
was ever better than before,
where names mix with the sound of machetes,
bayonets, bullets, this music, this bloody
bombastic order
of our days.

OTHER THAN FULLNESS

All their flowers have left me.
Even their old words are walking away,
just as it must be for the bell to leave its foundry,
for the peal to leave its bell.

There was a bell a block from my house,
in the monsignor's castle, and as a girl I would hear
it ring the hour in the slow unraveling night,
and some days, I would visit the emptiness it hung above,
and climb the stone steps to solitude
where I'd genuflect and kneel, and what I liked best
was the holy water in marble fonts, the dip and cross
on the way in, the dip and cross on the way out.

Now nights I wake to the train whistling, *I hear,*
I think, I say my name, singing.
Sometimes I rise to watch the street lighted by lampposts
with heads like sunflowers, but bowed
by a force other than fullness.
These, not the lyrical globes of my girlhood, whose lighting
meant it was time to go home.

The streetlights were how my mother
called us, silently, it's the way she still calls,
now that I've lost the sound of her voice, the sound
I would give all the transparency
in all my windows to get back, even as memory,
even dreaming, but asleep, instead of her words,
it's just my own voice that speaks, the voice
that last night announced to no one,
Abandonment certifies your heart with thunder.

THE LAST SKIN

Has anyone described the smell of wishbones drying
on the kitchen sill or the smell of glass, or the bucket of water
lifted from the well we go to when death takes the last thirst
from someone we love?

After my mother died, sometimes
I'd take the one piece of her clothing I'd kept
to bed and bury my face
in her flowered blouse to smell her last skin,
but even from the first it was futile.

What I got was the smell of goneness, the smell of screen
doors where moths have spent their wing powder
beating failingly to reach the light.

My massage therapist said she felt grief
in my body like hard empty boxes.
I felt like I was always handling dough,
never wanting the kneading to be done, never wanting
to bake the bread that meant the end of something having to do
with a mother and daughter in a kitchen.

My mother has been gone for years, and I begin to see,
in the spots on the backs of my hands, in the shelf
my cheekbones make for my cheeks, in the way I hold
my mouth against gravity's pull, that I carry her
with me, my skin, her skin,
her last skin.

PART II: LAKE TITICACA

• Lake Titicaca

At 12,500 feet, straddling the border between Peru and Bolivia, it's the highest lake in the world navigable by large ships. The name Titicaca has uncertain origins but has been translated variously to mean Rock of the Puma or Crag of Lead. It measures 120 miles at its longest point and 50 miles at its widest. The lake contains forty-one islands, some densely inhabited, some made out of grass. The lake's deepest point reaches to 920 feet. Peaks in the Cordillera Real on the Bolivian side of the lake rise to 21,000 feet and are among the highest mountains in the Andes. Some say the sun burns off more than 150,000 gallons of lake water per second.

WHY THE LAKE

Because so much water
gathered at such a height
that its majesty called,
just as the lake called to draw blue
out of the day's sky
and later the night's black.

Of course the sky drew
the lake out of itself,
at first invisibly
but then colorfully
so the sky could paint itself
white in places,
make mountains of grays,
and when too heavy to hold,
the sky let the lake go,
bit by wet bit in an unexpected
sparkling of droplets.

To be in that space
between the lake and the sky
was to be inside chanting,
desire made so celestial,
it stops.

FLOATING ISLANDS

Snowy peaks on the far shore no bigger than saw teeth,
the lake a bowl so cosmic it holds a constellation of islands—
Aymara here, Quechua there, and the Uros, who make
their islands out of reeds. For twenty-five days,
they row boatloads of tortora grass to throw down on the water,
until the mass becomes a flat nest dense enough to hold
houses, a museum, a church, all made out of the same stuff,
monochromatic villages of straw, odd at first, but then look
at the houses on the shores of the lake that rise
out of the dark chocolate earth, unpainted exterior walls
more bitter than sweet, so that you see
an entire town made unmistakably of dirt.
But on the floating islands, they've built a ten-foot flamingo
out of reeds so tourists like us can rise above the often squishy mat
that we know is rotting from the bottom but have no idea
how often more grass has to be thrown down to balance the decay,
and you wonder whether that means they have to move the museum
of dead birds and the church, with its unexpected candles,
and the flamingo, where up here we're waving now for the camera,
oblivious to the equation of how much grass will support
how much weight, or which straw will be the last.

BLUE DOOR

The thin air slows me down, and I stop on the dirt road
to stare at whatever is there when I'm winded.
Here a cow chews lugubriously, and I'm almost close
enough to hear its stomach drumming
out of beat with the thumping of its edible heart, and the breath
rushing in and out of lungs the size of small tents.
From the house beside the cow, a boy appears and closes
the blue door behind him, so we can't see
the man and the woman sitting silently
on unpainted chairs at an unpainted table
that will probably never in its life span of plates
bear the weight of more than one or two books,
and between the thatched roof and the dirt floor
the man thinks about their son, how much longer before his voice
changes and he can leave school, and the woman thinks about
how soon she'll be able to cook the long slab of the cow's tongue,
while outside I take a picture of the boy in front of the blue door,
the boy grinning in that spendthrift way of the young,
happy he doesn't have to look up at the roof of the house and worry
how long before the rotting grass will have to be re-thatched,
and he doesn't have to look down at the dirt floor that will always
be dirt, despite daily sweepings, and he grins because he knows
how to row in a wooden boat with oars like condor wings,
and someday he'll row out into the wide watery meadow
at the lake's edge like the couple he watched this morning—
a slightly older kid he knows and a girl with x's on her stocking cap,
their boat getting smaller and smaller in the tortora grass,
the kid rowing until the lances of green enclose them,
the way my camera captures the boy posing in front of his house,
thinking about this tourist lady, and what could she possibly know
beyond a door, the color of a little bit of heaven
with some darkness added, and the right amount of oil
to make it shine.

MANAGER OF THE EMPTY HOTEL

You can tell he's in exile, living here by the lake
the way a chandelier inhabits a condemned ballroom.
He stares out at the vastness, but doesn't see
old wounds rearranging themselves in its waters.

He paces a lot, lamenting his lost step, maybe
his standing in another job, something to do
with armed guards and flying cash to the capital.
All his workers speak in native tongues,
and he can't stop them, any more than he can quiet his wife,
who fears water and talks like a river that will never be broken.

We are the only guests, making our stay here like a visit
with relatives, cousins so far removed we've forgotten
how the bloodline took another fork in the road,
leading to this isolated spot on a spit of land,
where no one arrives but the three of us, like lost family.

To answer our questions, the manager picks at random
as if from a deck of cards and rattles off a rehearsed reply
that pretends to be generous but isn't. He says,
There are no pumas in the hills, but he has the look
of someone who's seen them at his door in the dead of night,
each extended claw casting a shadow in the dimness of starlight.

THE LAKE'S AIR

You could drown in this air, the way wanting
what you can't get enough of so bad
makes you gasp. This thinness, not far from glass—
how easy it is to look through until it breaks
apart.

~⁹

Breathlessness like a kind of blindness,
the air so empty, the light so sharp, the sun
swaggering above the dazzling everywhere
of the lake, we're held here,
holding still, conserving
the painted air, until we can see again.

~⁹

You can long for the courtly.
You can ache for the coupling of souls.
You can undo it all in a heartbeat,
the way our one star wagers pails of its light
on the lake.

~⁹

Look at the horizon, the blue hugging
the blue.
It is okay to beg, to plead for
the blue
to descend like a fix,
until we're besotted with breath.

TOWN OF ORPHANED TEETH

You can bet there's a Christ on the hill,
looking down on the town, his arms outstretched,
balanced evenly, as if he couldn't imagine
weighing the kids dazed on glue against
the drivers of the monster jeeps, their glass darkened
to distance the streets that look like churned-up mud and blood,
or to weigh the women with babies on their laps, begging
for the local money called "suns," against the tourists
who steal their pictures with digital cameras.
I confess, I don't want to give up my Toyota Corolla
so kids here don't have to go barefoot in the dirt, but I keep asking
what Jesus delivers, watching over a town of empty mouths,
some with a few orphaned teeth still chewing coca leaves,
a town where everyone is in bed with the gods,
all of them slumbering over this forsaken place, even
the god on the hill, who sleeps with a hammer.

WINDOWS ON THE LAKE

From this wall of windows, the lake stretches hugely,
as if trying to reach beyond the ghost of a chance.
Ducks fly in twos and threes. Myself,
I'm on the lookout for the small black birds,
with gold coins hidden under wing and tail feathers
so it's not until they fly that you see
their bright yellow secrets.

How far will a bird hop on ground before choosing
flight, and how long can I sit here with my memories
pinging incoherently off the glass like bugs
trying to find a way out?

I keep thinking of my poet friend channeling
D. H. Lawrence and making poems like nesting dolls.
Even the smallest could hold the whole lake, its pink trout,
the runoff from the mines turning the shore
a sick green, and boats with sails
made from feed sacks, reminding me
of my mother's beige purse, her last, and the few
things I kept—her tape measure and the scissors
she used for more than fifty years, having them sharpened
and resharpened, until one day without knowing it
she'd made her last cut.

At the lake, it's New Year's Eve day, and the women here
are racing rowboats, heading toward us and the rock
out our window they'll round, nuggets of color
getting bigger as they approach, the race
making me think of my father and the sacredness
of Saturday afternoon horses, this downs,
then that, and the dream that a two-dollar bet would pay off,
and how the only time I went with him to the track, I bet
tens and twenties in yet another childish one-upping,

and him so weak he could barely breathe, let alone yell at me,
while I bet on horses like Heaven Help Us, Gone But Not Forgotten,
Angel Baby, names that made me think of my mother,
who I felt still hovering around me, and my horses,
winners, every one, and my father stupefied,
because in his view what did I know about anything.

Back at the lake my daughter says let's bet on the boats,
ten soles each, because of the endearing upside-down plane
on the back of the bill, but the race ends the way it began,
in the order of the three in front at the start, too much
like life to be fun, so we wonder if the winners
are wearing yellow panties,
a custom here at New Year's for good luck, sold from
stacks and stacks of yellow his and hers
and bought yearly the way my father bought
his one lottery ticket a week, indignant
when he didn't win.

Just now the young boy who yesterday
rowed by in the boat named Ben Hur arrives at the window
to beg for a pencil, and I want to ask
if the people here have a special language for lake shine,
its various embellishments of light, the kind of words
like *finish line, jackpot, somewhere over the rainbow,*
you might want to hold before you die.

IT CAME DOWN ICE LAST NIGHT

And this night now
far from the ire of men
far from the veins of women
and their fast elbows
there is lightning in Bolivia.

Across the dark water
far from our desperate talk
and the lake's obsessive licking,
explosions soberly ignite the far clouds
and with each flash—
the faces we have touched
and lost,
their eyes mute now
in memory.

Thunder shakes us like the dreams
that build strange architecture in our sleep—
white stones, red walls, room
after room catching in your throat.

But above us here in clear skies
there are stars that could keep us
from staring into the storm,
from bloodying ourselves
over and beyond the call of beauty.

PART III

IRISES OF KRAKÓW

Irises bloomed blithely in the Botanical Garden,
petals performing new experiments

in beauty, as if an entire circus had been
melted down—trapezists, monkey hats,

elephant masks, even the *oooohs* and *aaaahs*
of the audience—all captured, recast in a crazy variety of tongues.

We walked without talking, numb
to their braggadocios, their arias, their manic flutes.

I wanted to surrender to their beauty,
craving some nature beyond human.

If their names appeared on small signs,
we didn't read them, letting their identities go

reeling away like the lengths of knotted scarves
magicians pull out of nowhere, gone like peasants

picked off by fever, the ones that took
the long names and short lives of both

my great-grandparents, dying weeks apart
in the one room of their house.

I thought then of my great-uncles, Sunday dinners,
on North Street, America, how they sliced

ghastly slabs of gleaming fat off the smoked
shoulder. None of them would have visited a garden,

fleeing as they had the dirt floor of their Polish past.
Neither would they have visited the camp we'd just come from,

its silent dunes of hair, dumps of eyeglasses,
prosthetic limbs, valises, the horror of what was hoarded

speaking the absence of the lives and lives and lives
discarded,

and if my Polish uncles lived now, I would tell them what I saw,
I would rage until they wept away their hatreds,

or else weep myself, letting my tears fall on their hands,
their cheeks, on their awful stubborn ignorance.

AT THE RUSSIAN SAMOVAR

In the half-light on the second floor, empty but for us,
we rearranged tables many times, inexplicably
moving them like map pieces that might align Uzbekistan
with Azerbaijan, Kubla Khan with Purgistan.
Herring was served on platters the blue of Russia's
White Sea, or call it the color of asters.
We poured vodka into small glasses
with waists, while below us the bar crowd carried on
like a crew loyal only to testosterone.
Did anyone else feel safe from the long lash of time,
or was it just me, in love with the poets (who wasn't a poet?)
and with my dearest—dashing in his topcoat from Goodwill.
Talk flew like sparrows and once in a while silence held forth
to make room for pierogi with mushrooms,
and laughing chased away moths and remnants of worry rags,
though each of us held on not very secretly to a few shreds.
Some swayed in the direction of a joke,
others leaned toward a bit of gossip.
Dragging up a chair to flirt with L, the waiter claimed
to study zoology, the big cats, and went on (why?)
to quote Herodotus, who thought the lioness
expels her whole womb upon her one birth.
"Sounds to me like writing," said E,
and we ordered more vodka in new flavors—
horseradish, cranberry—and everyone
drank to health, to long life, and I drank, too, in hopes
that no one from my past would appear
to banish me and claim my place at the table.

AN OXCART AND THE AROMA OF HAZELNUTS

Once you reach the cliff's drop,
you remember the trumpeter
and how on the hour his fanfare broke
before the last notes, beautiful precipitous
endings, to mark time and remind you
to rejoice.

Once you reach the sea's edge
you remember the monks
who poured milk, then brilliantly colored sand
into the river to let their mandala of a palace
flow out into the wildest waters, into the sound
of the ocean that will always be the earth's breathing,
rushing in, rushing out.

Once you reach the end of the street
you will remember the bird fancier
who lived for a time on the fourth floor
above the shop marked by the head of a rhino,
there in your grandmother's country
where she warned: Don't call the wolf
out of the forest.

When you reach the top of the mountain
you will be at the end, because in life
you were too fat and lazy to climb such heights,
but look—the sun will be weightless and the rain silky,
and if you want, there'll be an oxcart and the aroma of hazelnuts,
feathers of the glossiest birds, and a necklace of string,
blessed by the breath of the highest holiness,
and each strand will tie you to your life's happiest times,
the ones you crowded out
by your wanton rehearsals of hurts.

EAVESDROPPING

"Cast the net wide," he says, his voice stagey, modulated
by self-importance—*the too-good-to-be-true syndrome*—here in
a hotel restaurant, where he's talking too loudly for the loneliness
of the room and me trying to read poetry over breakfast,
but the poems are no match for his namedropping recognizable
first names, using them the way a guy would suck a toothpick
defiantly during dessert, or the way another man—
it's not the people at your throat, it's the people at your elbow—
would wear a gold chain on darkly tanned skin, two shirt buttons
more than you want to see, and this calls up
the mortician on Oakland Boulevard, a slimeball
who could have been Eddie Haskell in another life before getting in
over his head with the greyhounds, hiding out now in a mortuary,
and besides the too-muchness of his tan and chest hair, the final straw
was how his mouth's attempt at decorum failed
in a half-cocked smirk that presided over our talk
about my mother's remains.
Lies, what do they get you—
a broken heart, says the voice two tables away, a debatable point,
but he's still got the three guys with him rapt.
You don't know what it's like to see you, I said. Why
aren't you dead? The waiter is desperate—*stranded on an iceberg*—
to punch out for the day, but the voice is winding up to Jack this, Fidel that,
and *I saw Jackie on Madison Ave., and before I could say hello, she said, I know,*
I know. Then it's on to Mort this, Garrison that, and Peter Dale Scott,
who, despite his JFK books, takes me to Kraków and Milosz,
the Skalka Sanctuary's underground crypt where he rests,
how I wished I'd brought flowers when I stood over his massive stone tomb,
feeling a heartbreak I felt unentitled to, puzzling
again over the line "death is the mother of beauty," but the voice blows hard
into my reverie—*It never pays off. Those morons, just a gorilla band,*
which I spelled like that in my mind, thinking big apes with flutes and drums,
playing dismally—*to work the chow line*—and now of course I see

it was guerrilla band and the last words I heard
after *White House* were *They've got blood on their hands*
and it emboldens them.

THE HEAD

Cast-metal sculpture, Market Square, Kraków

We, who knew nothing of the language there, unable
to speak the name of a single bread, stood in thrall
to its self-sufficiency, its grand oblivion.

Silence surrounded us and went beyond to ghost
the colonnades, where once maybe a man stirred ashes,
and a maid, too poor for perfume, stewed roses.

It lay sideways, an ear to the ground,
and its emptiness exhaled the truths and lies of secrets—
breezes sighing across fields of rapeseed ripened yellow,

heralds gathering all the answers to all the questions buried
under each of the stones that had cobbled the square
for centuries and centuries.

From the head's hollow, memories echoed, too, wrapping us
in ancient shawls, and we could feel the grandmothers in them,
their hands weaving wools that would be clutched

for ages of fevers, other cloth that filled with blood
when bullets in a forest eased through them
and into bodies falling into mass graves.

Bands wrapped the head, as if someone from a castle
had brought bindings, battered bridles, perhaps,
and though circling the face, they left the nose free

that it might breathe, the mouth free to hold its own kiss,
the holes meant for eyes free to be holes,
holes beyond ransom, beyond sainthood,

and from their blindness poured great hordes
fleeing across the steppes, famines at the end of winter
after the last potato was cut, Cossacks

riding recklessly into village after village
their boots made of fearful lengths of leather,
swords and swords and swords.

PICNICKING WHERE THE PONY RIDES USED TO BE

It must have been spring and Forest Park
must have been earning its name, trees greening
everywhere with the frailness that new leaves use
to create a featheriness that's disarming.
The sun must have burned through the moist of morning
since the ground was warm, and our stories spilled out
like prehistory that happened to people we didn't know,
and the hardest parts felt like they belonged on another planet.
Around us the spirits of ponies tip-tapped the dirt,
keeping time with the pleadings of childhood,
which now after thirty years, we know keep on plodding
through our lives the way the ponies circled the small ring,
where we picnicked with Saint André, apples, and crackers,
and strewn about us, abandoned saddle blankets
almost camouflaged in the dirt reminded us
of the paltry renting for a few pennies a small share of creature life,
the pony smell rising up, hot, mixed with the rankness
of droppings, while two beings rode round and round
trapped in a ring,
                    like a distant ring circled by people,
and though long ago, I remember the headband I wore—
fake pearls glued together on a plastic arch—
and the red broadcloth dress with white shell buttons on the bodice
fitted at the waist, and the skirt's flare—that Sunday my father
(or was it the pony man?) lifted me onto a waiting back,
and before my time was up, something inside the beast
seized, causing the pony to rise up on hind legs, bucking
and clawing the air with its front, to throw me,
before I knew it, backside in the dirt,
shamed by my failure and worried
about how many had seen how much of my panties
as I was hurled smack-dab back
into the bit and bridle of childhood.

DEAR C

Can I lure you back in touch, even if only voice to voice
squeezed into wires that travel as you so memorably wrote
under miles and miles of sleeping birds' feet?
Do you remember the high reaches of Point Reyes we walked
and how the grass sparkled, frenzied by the wind striking

the headland, almost pushing us back down the path,
while the wild irises bowed but didn't break?
And the day we drove the width of California to walk
Limantour at sunset and pause on the beach
at an empty seal, flattened on the sand?

All I can remember about the inn in Inverness
where we ate is the bread and wine, made
by adding a single-celled fungus yeast to dough and grapes,
how mixing an animal thing with a vegetable
creates a third.

A mix like that could transform speechlessness
into sound, but your silence has grown longer and longer.
Sometimes I hear it as if a stranger were raking the grass,
raking up leaves fallen off the ash
into asymmetrical pillows.

After more than three decades of friendship, remember
turning thirty, forty, fifty, and how many of the dates
we celebrated with poems and mischief? Sometimes silence
feels like an easy truce between your madness to reel in and my
madness to reel out,

but now I'm in an empty field waving a white handkerchief
at you over a great distance. Sometimes the emptiness
feels like ground so parched even the worms have died.

Remember how, sleeping lightly in Death Valley, I'd wake
to tell you one-second dreams?

And the thunder egg we found laid by the thunder chicken
that brings the rains to the land where we met,
driving aimlessly, like feathers on a wind, through forests
in wetness and mists, talking, never idling,
never stalling?

I've forgotten how we freed the falcon in your backyard
stuck between the fence and a bush.
Wasn't it strangely easy, despite the bird's desperate flapping,
how with no hesitation or wounds, we helped it
fly away?

DRIVING TO X IN TEXAS

The wind was wild. You kept saying, "Hold back
from the road," the kind of incoherent command my father
gave me decades ago during driving lessons.
Longhorn cattle chased a truck along the feeder road.
An armadillo scuttled into the dust, and I wondered
if its penis was in fact six feet long in human terms, as I'd read.
I know two pieces of armadillo shell can be sewn
with twine to make a bag like the one I bought in Tierradentro
and hung on my study wall to remind me of traveling far,
unlike this local cruising, not talking, listening
to a Górecki string quartet, music that could come only
from a country claimed and reclaimed
from history's lost-and-found,
the strings articulating the past, its carnage, its rue,
difficult music, interrupted by a parade
of lambs and sheep trotting across a field, where midway,
a fawn had fallen into step, just another bit
from the road's cabinet of wonders,
which every few miles held huge white monoliths.
Humongous chalk to draw the woolly clouds in the severe clear
or towering salt licks for some gargantuan ungulate we had yet to meet?
Animals kept appearing, as if someone ahead
had yelled, "Cue up the weasel," and upon our arrival,
it dashed in front of our car.
When we reached the turnoff for the town of Whon,
I asked myself who, what, when, where, whon,
summing up the wanness of belonging nowhere,
an exile like the letter "x" left out
of the Polish alphabet, and after years of rambling,
I thought, wow, now Texas, where a snake had crawled
across a hot road and died, yesterday a symbol,
today a belt.

AUJOURD'HUI

When I asked the entomologist, she said the tiniest
of the tiny was called an angel, or a fraction, but possibly
I misheard, willfully, the way my husband this morning
woke while I was reading a book, or rather not reading
but watching a speck of life emerge from the spine
and float across the page the way a dust mote floats
across a slice of sunlight slanting into a room.
The mite slides almost leglessly on slivers of slivers of hair,
on the faintest, if any, breath, leaving its cavernous lair
in the binding to crawl among words.
This parcel of parsed blood, dwarfed by the dot
of the i on the page, proceeds, an ambitious monk
the color of cayenne, trusting I'll resist
the impulse to touch.
Because we have no idea of its life span, let's call it
Aujourd'hui, a name long enough to hide in, unseen
by my husband, who, having risen from another page,
has appeared, a white largeness at the door.
To my news that his hair is standing straight up on end
he responds, "It's a bird thing. I'm practicing
to be a cockatoo."

PALM READING

Give me your whole hand so it opens
the way dreams bloom at night.
That line points to your hometown, it's shaped
like the blade of a skate. You left behind
everything but carry with you a dread of thin ice
and the deepest fear of melting.
Look here how lust deepens the line between your palm
and your thumb, that opposable digit you used to hitch
a ride to the next car, the next backseat, the next
you-know-what. In all the tiny razor lines—there—
your oldest friend, time. Notice the capital letter M.
Remember that—we'll get to it later. But first,
thirst. At the base of your pinkie
you have a water tower etched on this little pad,
unfortunately an unquenchable sign. Don't worry.
On the tower I can make out the letters NOA—
not overly aggressive, neglecting overt anxiety, or
not over anger. Don't mind. Stretch your palm out
until your tendons feel like they are skydiving.
Breathe like you own the right to some new air.
I can tell that you do not pray much but like your mother
you are good at opening jars. There will be fewer
and fewer fireflies in your future, but this loss, I fear,
you share with the entire world.
Here, the scar of an ancient wart.
Do your best to ignore it. If you look at it too long
espíritus malignos might enter your body at this point.
Roads. Many, many roads. Ask yourself why
you sighed when I said this. Perhaps it's the dream
of a country that begins with O. Maybe the moon
of your future will rise lackadaisically in this country,
or should I say languorously? Words,
not for me like truth written on the skin.
Make a little cup with your hand. Do this when

you want to beg, but only beg for what can fill
this empty little cave. What?
No, I am not a Buddhist. I am a gypsy, my eyes
see everything, not nothing.
We have to end soon. Realize
from my perspective the big M is a big W.
This means you wish too much.
Imagine now the way a wind waves its way
through a field of tall grass and how each blade
bends alone in its own time, but together
they make the wind visible.
                         Grass, lines, letters—
all mystery. Hold on to it.

SWEET GLUE

Though now my darling and I prance with abandon
in the walking lane of the Incarnate Word pool
to vary our plodding for our bad backs,
and though at other times, we have bounded together
toward boundlessness, recapitulating the life cycle of a camellia,
from wrapped bud to petal-fall,
and though I have felt the slow opening
from O to O to O to O
that let a new life slide into its own name,
and though a plane landing on a frozen river,
and a house in the tropics through which butterflies flew
as commonly as spiders the size of saucers climbed the walls,
and though at least a dozen earthquakes and many Northern Lights,
the sky seizing and catapulting with sherbet and candy,
and though joy and dread, twin shadows, have followed me
forever, and looking back, I could see them boxing each other,
and though half a lifetime is over, I still weirdly miss the weekly
teenage dances in dark halls,
                              body to body
melting together like gas into flame, burning
at the edge of eternal questions that in fact
we could not have cared less about, bent
as we were on the songs' sweet glue that bound us length
to length, our feet virtually stuck to the floor while we draped
our weight on each other in a bond adults would call filthy,
but was really only lostness clinging to lostness,
confused hope shaping our befuddled
minds and our bold wants popping out of nowhere,
so we clung fast, to slow down
the speeding up carrying us faster
than we wanted to travel toward that awful word
adulthood,
crouched like a lumbering animal inside us,

omnivorous eater of berries, worms, and bones,
its ambush unimaginable,
but certain.

VENTRILOQUISM

When I saw the face of a clock, the broken heirloom from some uncle,
reflected in a mirror across the room I thought, Now *this*
is nostalgia, so why go back again and again to the water
on that morning in Berkeley I woke before dawn in a hotel on the bay,
not in the Grant Street house, home for a dozen years and now astonishingly
another's for another dozen, all of them flying,

                               that morning I circled
the great looping path at Waterfront Park, retracing steps I'd walked a lot,
the way I sometimes trace the still face of my mother in framed photos,
there was something about the ducks sleeping on the inland channel,

                             maybe they'd slept on medallions
the moon made spilling itself on smooth sheets before sun and the wind
conspired to shatter the surface into millions of pennies,

                            that made me want to be a duck,
to belong to a luck of ducks, my iridescent head hidden under a wing
while I slept and floated toward shore and then paddled back to a safer
distance, sleeping and paddling with my fellow ducks,

                            then later on the bay side I wished
I could sit on one of the benches forever, watching the fog come and go
in the Golden Gate and the bridge a mere filament lacing the two headlands—
from that distance sea lions lazing on the horizon—

                            but if this is where I used to come
often to escape anger, to lick my wounds, to dwell on broken promises,
many my own, some to myself, leading to more misery and flagellation
echoed by the water hitting the rocks that it needs to create that slapping
sound,

                            why do I return,
is it nostalgia for nostalgia, or am I looking for something I lost,
the way my dog in Texas, shorn for the summer, kept sniffing
the wastebasket that held her clippings and would look up
as if to ask, "Where am I?"

                            Because time heals all wounds,
I'm happy to see the clock face doubled in the mirror that I gleefully
bought back for a quarter at the yard sale of the friend I'd given it to

some Christmas before, because I so loved the wooden frame,
a miniature of a window in a Gothic cathedral.
                                        But what surprises me in the photo
I took that day at the marina is the chalky white X, in the foreground,
each arm as long as a horse, a mark
I had never noticed before, and I have no idea
if it was put there as a target or if it's the remnant of a love letter,
the rest gone, just the anonymous kiss I wish
had been mine.

PIGEONS, A LOVE POEM

The pigeons are back, shitting and laughing in the eaves,
gangs landing out of reach, laughing
the way I once laughed so fast my mouthful of wine
flew across the table onto my friend and his funny story,
and in the pigeons' laughter we can hear liquid gurgling,
dumbly defying your latest invention, a motion-activated
sound machine that made a mechanical wheeze
every time a bird landed, and yes, the pigeons fled
the noise of what sounded like a motorized heart,
lurching in the direction of life, but when I complained
that the on/off of an artificial heart left me breathless,
you gave up on the deterrence of sound and set to work
on a silent water-shooting device, bringing water
up to the second-floor porch with a garden hose,
which looked to me like a code violation, snaking
up against the swami yellow of our clapboards,
and as you perfected the ultimate pigeon banishment,
a board flew out of your hands,
the way the wine flew from my mouth, the way pigeons
flew from that made-up groaning heart, and in the same
way my wine landed on Dave's shirt, your board landed
on Billye's convertible parked in the driveway next door,
ripping through the canvas top, and even though this
was the second board to make the flight
from your hands to her car (last time the hood),
and though for the price of our homeowner's deductible
we could have hired a guy to sit on the porch for a short
eternity to shoot the last pigeon into Kingdom Come,
I laughed harder than the time I spit the wine, I laughed
over and over, passionately, enough to waste
a bottle's worth of airborne Bordeaux, and because your hands
have held on to me for more than thirty years, never
slipping, never letting go, what's a couple of boards over the edge
and what's love, if not this?

ONCE THE OCEAN TAKES YOU

The ocean grants you absolution or it floods you
with sin. Either way it cleanses itself, water
rushing toward bigger water.

Fish water, whale water, water of barnacles, starfish,
and salt, water gleaming through ages
of starlight, moonlight, sunlight,
and hiding most of itself in the dark.

Once the ocean takes you, it's over. You can gaze
all you want into the distance, but nothing else consoles,
just the huge restlessness of water in which you see
all your past, all your time to come, all the questions
about what makes love like sand, its infinity of drifts
and shapes, close up its cosmos of debris and sparkle,
nothing but the blue horizon in its umpteen blues,
all calling you to where you belong,
at the ocean's edge, feeling at peace,
understanding nothing.

EXERCISING A VERB SELDOM USED IN THE FIRST PERSON

I pardon fastness and lassitude and the wind
for its erratic illness, I pardon
hope for facing off against hope,
I pardon Sundays in the long-ago, their hours
as long as whale songs,
I pardon my ancestors for being landless,
and squirrels for their rodent ways and wearing boas
at the wrong end, I pardon literalness and
fear of flying, fear of diving, fear of spiders,
because I've never had them, but once
in the Manuel Antonio house I smashed a spider
the size of a fist and its liquid splattered the skin
of my arms and legs, and it was fearsome and unforgettable.
I pardon knowledge for its impossible vastness
and the God particle for its infinitesimal infinitude,
and the bureau of time for defining
the exact hour of twilight. I pardon scientists
for harvesting fog, but science brings up too many
numbers after the decimal point, so excuse me
if I go back to my own anxiety,
which I pardon for its namelessness, but not for its
clammy grip. I pardon, you pardon, he/she/it pardons
my lost friend, for hopscotching out of the lines,
and never, not once, looking back.
I pardon whoever left the mess of sequin hearts
on the living room rug, because holding one in my hand
distracts me from the next pardon,
the hardest, to pardon my mother for dying
before I arrived, and I pardon her, too,
for leaving her last pulse
to let me know I was *that* close.
And as for you, Henry, not yet, I thought at the start,
it wasn't in me to pardon you, but now, having practiced,
why not, why not do it, Dad,

pardon you, pardon me,
your hullabaloos, my grudges,
your muteness, your blasphemy
your blustering, my defiance.
So here then I pardon you
for never moving past anger on the list of emotions,
pardon you your cage,
pardon you for not knowing how to love
the inevitable company
we made together in our misery.

IMPOSSIBLE DANCE

Standing at the window, at a loss,
I listened to the radio left playing next door
in the house long vacant, the music vacant, too,
so hollow I could supply my own song,
but what came instead was a vision,
clear balloons of jellyfish
sailing through the airiest water,
transparency held aloft in transparency,
tender animate emptiness propelled
by tentacles and sighs.

After they took my mother's shell
to the place it would burn,
I remade her bed and lay there,
wild, pinning
myself to her last place.
Her air—all I wanted was her air.

Five years later to the day, again I go
through the stations of grief, death's awful
offices, a dance that is never learned, or ever done,
only sorrow, my invisible partner, yanking me
in tune to an orchestra always out of earshot,
somewhere beyond belief.

WASHING THE ELEPHANT

Isn't it always the heart that wants to wash
the elephant, begging the body to do it
with soap and water, a ladder, hands,
in tree-shade big enough for the vast savannahs
of your sadness, the strangler fig of your guilt,
the cratered full moon's light fueling
the windy spooling memory of elephant?

What if Father Quinn had said, "Of course you'll recognize
your parents in heaven," instead of
"Being one with God will make your mother and father
pointless." That was back when I was young enough
to love them absolutely though still fear for their place
in heaven, imagining their souls like sponges full
of something resembling street water after rain.

Still my mother sent me every Saturday to confess,
to wring the sins out of my small baffled soul, and I made up lies
about lying, disobeying, chewing gum in church, to offer them
as carefully as I handed over the knotted handkerchief of coins
to the grocer when my mother sent me for a loaf of Wonder,
Land O'Lakes, and two Camels.

If guilt is the damage of childhood, then eros is the fall of adolescence.
Or the fall begins there, and never ends, desire after desire parading
through a lifetime like the Ringling Brothers elephants
made to walk through the Queens-Midtown Tunnel
and down 34th Street to the Garden.
So much of our desire like their bulky, shadowy walking
after midnight, exiled from the wild and destined
for a circus with its tawdry gaudiness, its unspoken
pathos.

It takes more than half a century to figure out who they were,
the few real loves-of-your-life and how much of the rest—
the mad breaking-heart stickiness—falls away, slowly,
unnoticed, the way you lose your taste for things
like Popsicles unthinkingly.
And though dailiness may have no place
for the ones that have etched themselves in the laugh lines
and frown lines on the face that's harder and harder
to claim as your own, often one love-of-your-life
will appear in a dream, arriving
with the weight and certitude of an elephant,
and it's always the heart that wants to go out and wash
the huge mysteriousness of what they meant, those memories
that have only memories to feed them, and only you to keep them clean.

NOTES

Barbara Ras is the author of the poetry collections *Bite Every Sorrow* (LSU Press, 1998), chosen by C. K. Williams to receive the 1997 Walt Whitman Award and also awarded the Kate Tufts Discovery Award, and *One Hidden Stuff* (Penguin, 2006). Ras has received fellowships from the John Simon Guggenheim Memorial Foundation, the Artist Foundation of San Antonio, and the Bread Loaf Writers' Conference.

Her poems have appeared in the *New Yorker, TriQuarterly, American Scholar, Massachusetts Review, Orion*, as well as many other magazines and anthologies. She is the editor of a collection of short fiction in translation, *Costa Rica: A Traveler's Literary Companion* (Whereabouts Press, 1994).

She has taught at writers' conferences across the country and has been on the faculty of the MFA Program for Writers at Warren Wilson College.

Ras lives in San Antonio, where she directs Trinity University Press.

JOHN ASHBERY
Selected Poems
Self-Portrait in a Convex Mirror

TED BERRIGAN
The Sonnets

JOE BONOMO
Installations

PHILIP BOOTH
Selves

JIM CARROLL
Fear of Dreaming: The Selected Poems
Living at the Movies
Void of Course

ALISON HAWTHORNE
DEMING
Genius Loci
Rope

CARL DENNIS
New and Selected Poems 1974–2004
Practical Gods
Ranking the Wishes
Unknown Friends

DIANE DI PRIMA
Loba

STUART DISCHELL
Backwards Days
Dig Safe

STEPHEN DOBYNS
Velocities: New and Selected Poems,
*   1966–1992*

EDWARD DORN
Way More West: New and Selected
*   Poems*

AMY GERSTLER
Crown of Weeds: Poems
Dearest Creature
Ghost Girl
Medicine
Nerve Storm

EUGENE GLORIA
Drivers at the Short-Time Motel
Hoodlum Birds

DEBORA GREGER
Desert Fathers, Uranium Daughters

God
Men, Women, and Ghosts
Western Art

TERRANCE HAYES
Hip Logic
Lighthead
Wind in a Box

ROBERT HUNTER
Sentinel and Other Poems

MARY KARR
Viper Rum

WILLIAM KECKLER
Sanskrit of the Body

JACK KEROUAC
Book of Sketches
Book of Blues
Book of Haikus

JOANNA KLINK
Circadian

JOANNE KYGER
As Ever: Selected Poems

ANN LAUTERBACH
Hum
If In Time: Selected Poems, 1975–2000
On a Stair
Or to Begin Again

CORINNE LEE
PYX

PHILLIS LEVIN
May Day
Mercury

WILLIAM LOGAN
Macbeth in Venice
Strange Flesh
The Whispering Gallery

ADRIAN MATEJKA
Mixology

MICHAEL MCCLURE
Huge Dreams: San Francisco and Beat
*   Poems*

DAVID MELTZER
David's Copy: The Selected Poems of
*   David Meltzer*

CAROL MUSKE
An Octave above Thunder
Red Trousseau

ALICE NOTLEY
The Descent of Alette
Disobedience
In the Pines
Mysteries of Small Houses

LAWRENCE RAAB
The History of Forgetting
Visible Signs: New and Selected Poems

BARBARA RAS
The Last Skin
One Hidden Stuff

PATTIANN ROGERS
Generations
Wayfare

WILLIAM STOBB
Nervous Systems

TRYFON TOLIDES
An Almost Pure Empty Walking

ANNE WALDMAN
Kill or Cure
Manatee/Humanity
Structure of the World Compared to a
*   Bubble*

JAMES WELCH
Riding the Earthboy 40

PHILIP WHALEN
Overtime: Selected Poems

ROBERT WRIGLEY
Earthly Meditations: New and
*   Selected Poems*
Lives of the Animals
Reign of Snakes

MARK YAKICH
The Importance of Peeling Potatoes in
*   Ukraine*
Unrelated Individuals Forming a
*   Group Waiting to Cross*

JOHN YAU
Borrowed Love Poems
Paradiso Diaspora